bootstrap
branding™

Bootstrap
Branding

An Entrepreneur's Guide to Building a Brand With Limited Finances

Vickie L. VanHurley, Ph.D.

Bootstrap Branding: An Entrepreneur's Guide to Building a Brand With Limited Finances

table of contents

introduction

Congratulations on making the investment in your business! I was inspired by small businesses and business start-up owners to develop a vehicle to share the importance of branding and how it is the key to a successful business. I developed this workbook to answer important questions like What is branding? Why do I need it? How do I do it with very little money? How will it help my business?

Working in *Bootstrap Branding: An Entrepreneur's Guide to Building a Brand With Limited Finances* you will have a better understanding of branding and its importance to your business success. This workbook is designed to assist you with branding your business even on a small budget. This workbook will assist you with developing and managing your branding efforts for maximum results. Enjoy branding your business to success!

Dr. Vickie VanHurley,
The Design Doc

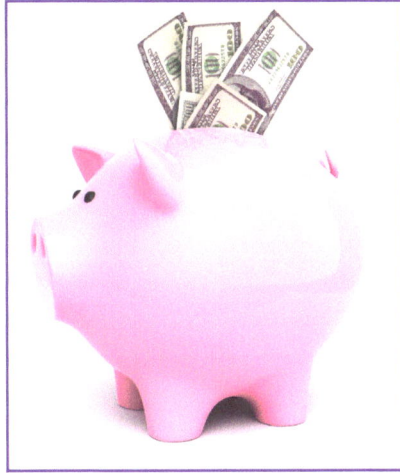

chapter 1

What is Bootstrapping?

According to Entrepreneur's Small Business Dictionary, bootstrapping is a situation in which an entrepreneur starts a business with little capital. This process is also known as self-funding. An entrepreneur is bootstrapping when he or she develops a business using personal finance. Compared to using loans from banks or investors, bootstrapping can be beneficial as the entrepreneur is able to maintain control over all decisions. Another benefit of bootstrapping is not waiting for someone else to determine when or if you start your business.

You are bootstrapping your dream (business, product, service) if you are:

❖ Using cash from savings

❖ Borrowing cash from family and friends

❖ Borrowing against assets, such as your home

❖ Carefully using selected credit cards

❖ Keeping your day job, while starting the business in off-hours

❖ Doing consulting work to provide start-up cash for the business and for living expenses

My mentor Dr. Stacia Pierce always says to "launch before you are ready" and self-funding provides the opportunity to launch. In other words, do not wait for "the perfect opportunity" to introduce your business, product, service to the world. However you must take time to look professional from the start.

Here are a few successful businesses that used bootstrapping to fund their start-up:

❖ Apple Inc.

❖ Clorox

❖ Facebook Inc.

❖ eBay Inc.

❖ Bare Naked Granola

❖ Mochi (Frozen Yogurt)

❖ Spanx (Shapewear)

❖ MailChimp (email Marketing Service)

❖ Craig's List

❖ Nasty Gal (Womens clothing, shoes, and accessories)

❖ Burt's Bees (Skincare and Beeswax Products)

chapter 2
What is Branding?

"Your brand is what others say about you when you're not in the room." ~Jeff Bezos, Founder of amazon.com

I'm sure everyone has heard of the word brand, and probably have spoken the word yourself. I'm sure we all have certain brands we buy or experience. Think of one of your favorite brands.

I'll start with this one: Coke. No other cola brand will do. There is **NO** substitution. I have witnessed people change their beverage order to water if the restaurant doesn't serve Coke. I also know people that will not go to a restaurant if they don't serve Coke products. Wow! That's brand loyalty! You can establish this type of brand loyalty for your product or service too!

Branding is NOT a logo. However it is difficult to establish a brand without one! Actually a logo is called a brand identifier and it is the "heart and soul" of a brand. Branding is about making the emotional connection. Branding is also the experience of using the product or service. Building a brand is similar to building a friendship. Consumers see a brand as an important part of a product and branding can add value to a product. Customers attach meaning to brands and develop brand relationships. For example: Tide laundry detergent. Created by Proctor & Gamble in 1943 and introduced to consumers in 1946. This brand is 70 years old and still going strong! Research has shown that Tide has established a relationship with its consumers. Tide has become a "generational" brand. Many Tide users state the reason they use Tide is because "my mom used it, and her mother used it", "I can trust Tide to get the grass stains out of my son's pants just like my mother used Tide to get the mud stains out of my dresses when I was his age" "My mother took pride with keeping us clean

My Favorite Brands ♥♥♥

Write down a few of your favorite brands. Make sure you write what makes it a favorite.

_____

_____

_____

_____

_____

_____

_____

_____

_____

_____

and happy. When I use Tide I feel like I'm keeping my family happy and clean." Proctor & Gamble has established a relationship with Tide users. A relationship that is past down through generations.

A Brand. According to *Entrepreneur's Small Business Dictionary,* your brand is your promise to your customer. It tells them what they can expect from your products, services, and it differentiates your offering from your competitors. Your brand is derived from who you are, who you want to be, and who people perceive you to be.

Your brand reflects the truth about your business and product.

Branding. It's about making the emotional connection. It is also the experience of using the product or service.

Every product or service (brand) has shoppers and consumers. Regardless of your product or service you are being shopped by potential consumers.

Building a brand is similar to building a friendship. Successful brands take time to discover who their shoppers are, what they like, and more importantly what they want. Like a friend, a brand caters to the likes, dislikes, and desires of the consumer.

The purpose of Branding. As a start-up no one knows you, your product, or service. Branding gives credibility to your business, product, or service. For small businesses it helps you stand out and compete. You MUST be seen to be considered by customers. Branding will help differentiate your business, product or service from your competitors. Consumers buy from a brand they know and trust!

chapter 3
Why Do I Need Branding?

Reason #1: As I mentioned in chapter one consumers buy from a brand they know and trust. When you are starting your business you are an unknown. This is similar to being the "new kid" at school. You find yourself walking into an established society of friends, groups, and new places. You have to constantly and consistently say "hello, my name is..." in order to be noticed. You have to hold a conversation with the person you are sitting next to in homeroom, science class, or at lunch. You are sharing your personality when you engage in conversations. You are providing opportunities for your new teachers and classmates to get to know your personality, your beliefs, your character. I have just simplified the branding process. You must do the same for your brand (business, product, or service).

Benefits of Branding:

❖ **Create awareness about your business, product, or service.** The more people see your brand, they will know it exists and consider buying your products, or services.

❖ **Consistency in the marketplace.** If branding is consistent the customer may perceive your product quality is consistent.

❖ **Recognition and Loyalty.** A strong brand name and logo helps to keep your business in the mind of potential customers.

❖ **Established Business.** People have a tendency to connect branding with larger businesses that have a generous budget dedicated to adverting and promotion. Strong branding, has the ability make your business appear to be much bigger than it really is.

❖ **Quality.** A strong brand projects an image of quality in your business. People view the brand as a part of a product or service with quality and value.

❖ **Experience.** A branded business is more likely to be viewed as experienced in their products or services. Your business, product, or service will be viewed as more reliable and trustworthy than an unbranded business.

Reason #2: Branding will help develop your promise (tag line) to your customers. It will keep you consistent with all you say and do. Branding provides a guideline and record of how you present your business, product, or service.

Benefits of Using a Tagline:

❖ Reveals if you have put any thought or effort into the mission of your business.

❖ Communicates that you have a clear direction or vision about what you offer.

❖ Gives your business a personality and it communicates your purpose.

Reason #3: **You can't afford NOT to brand!** You **MUST** invest in your business. If you are not willing to invest in your business, why should anyone invest in your business by buying your product or using your service? I'm reminded of the old saying "it takes money to make money!" It doesn't have to be a large sum of money. Good branding can be done with items from your favorite office supply store and favorite arts and crafts store with as little as $50 and your time and effort (sweat equity). Don't be afraid to ask for help. It's perfectly acceptable to create branding with your personal computer and a few items from your local office supply store and your favorite arts and craft store! I will talk about this more in Chapter 5: Ready, Set, Brand!

Notes

_____

_____

_____

_____

_____

_____

_____

_____

_____

_____

_____

_____

_____

_____

Bootstrap Branding: An Entrepreneur's Guide to Building a Brand With Limited Finances

Doodles page

Bootstrap Branding: An Entrepreneur's Guide to Building a Brand With Limited Finances

chapter 4
How to Build Your Branding Plan

Find three brands you are absolutely passionate about. You **LOVE** everything about this brand, product, or service. I will call these "Branding Success Examples." Find logos, pictures of products, packaging, tags, shopping bags and paste them on the Branding Success Example sheets. A great way to develop your branding plan and brand your way to success is by following a successful example.

Branding Plan Foundation Questions:
1. Why do you (why did you) want to start a business?

_____

_____

_____

_____

Bootstrap Branding: An Entrepreneur's Guide to Building a Brand With Limited Finances

2. What is your product or service?

_____

_____

3. What is the mission of your business?

_____

_____

_____

_____

_____

4. What is the name of your business?

_____

_____

5. What does the name of your business mean?

_____

_____

_____

6. How does your business, product, or service make someone's life easier, more enjoyable?

_____

_____

_____

_____

_____

_____

_____

_____

_____

_____

_____

_____

_____

Notes

Bootstrap Branding: An Entrepreneur's Guide to Building a Brand With Limited Finances

Doodles page

Branding Success Examples

Find logos, pictures of products, packaging, tags, shopping bags, etc. of your three brands and paste them below. Write comments about your "I Love It" moments (involvement with the brand). For example when you receive a coupon in your mailbox, a text message for a new or free product, see a TV or magazine advertisement.

paste logos, products, packaging, tags, shopping bags, etc. of brand #1 here

Name of Brand or Product: _____

I LOVE It Moment! ♥♥♥

_____

_____

_____

_____

_____

Branding Success Examples

Find logos, pictures of products, packaging, tags, shopping bags, etc. and paste them below. Write comments about your "I Love It" moments (involvement with the brand). For example when you receive a coupon in your mailbox, a text message for a new or free product, see a TV or magazine advertisement.

paste logos, products, packaging, tags, shopping bags, etc. of brand #2 here

Name of Brand or Product: _____

I LOVE It Moment! ♥♥♥

_____

_____

_____

_____

_____

Branding Success Examples

Find logos, pictures of products, packaging, tags, shopping bags, etc. and paste them below. Write comments about your "I Love It" moments (involvement with the brand). For example when you receive a coupon in your mailbox, a text message for a new or free product, see a TV or magazine advertisement.

paste logos, products, packaging, tags, shopping bags, etc. of brand #3 here

Name of Brand or Product: _____

I LOVE It Moment! ♥♥♥

_____

_____

_____

_____

_____

Bootstrap Branding: An Entrepreneur's Guide to Building a Brand With Limited Finances

Business Naming Tips:
❖ Combination of names (yours, family, friends), a combination of favorite things, a description of your business, product, or service
❖ Easy to pronounce
❖ Easy to spell but in a unique way

The Branding Plan

1. Branding Objective

This is where you tell what your business, product, or service is about to do. Branding is about changing minds. An objective is something specific you want to accomplish. You may consider a branding objective as how you're going to change customers' minds about the obstacles that are preventing them from buying your product.

_____

_____

_____

_____

_____

_____

_____

_____

2. Brand Promise

Your brand promise is what customers will receive when they experience or use your product or service **EVERY** time! Complete each step to create your brand promise.

Brand Promise Foundation

Answer each question thoroughly. It may take time and a bit of research. Complete each section before moving to the next one!

❖ Why did I start this business, product, or service?

_____

_____

_____

_____

_____

_____

_____

_____

_____

_____

_____

Who Are My Competitors?

Find businesses that offer similar products and services that you offer. This will help you determine how you differ, what is special about your product or service. **Focus on three.**

Place Business #1 Logo or Picture of Product Here

Name of Business or Product:

_____

Website:_____

Physical Address (if any):

_____

_____

What is their claim to their customer (faster, bigger, smaller, cheaper, etc.)?

_____

_____

_____

_____

How is my product or service different? _____

_____

_____

_____

_____

Who Are My Competitors?

Find businesses that offer similar products and services that you offer. This will help you determine how you differ, what is special about your product or service.

Place Business
#2 Logo or
Picture of
Product Here

Name of Business or Product:

_____

Website:_____

Physical Address (if any):

_____

_____

What is their claim to their customer (faster, bigger, smaller, cheaper, etc.)?

_____

_____

_____

_____

How is my product or service different? _____

_____

_____

_____

_____

_____

Who Are My Competitors?

Find businesses that offer similar products and services that you offer. This will help you determine how you differ, what is special about your product or service.

Place Business #3 Logo or Picture of Product Here

Name of Business or Product:

_____

Website: _____

Physical Address (if any):

_____

_____

What is their claim to their customer (faster, bigger, smaller, cheaper, etc.)?

_____

_____

_____

_____

How is my product or service different? _____

_____

_____

_____

_____

What Does My Product or Service Do Well?

Think about why you started your business, product or service. List 5 things that you do differently or better than your competitors. For example, do you target a specific group or market? Does your product or service help those with special needs? Do you offer customization?

1. _____

_____

2. _____

_____

3. _____

_____

4. _____

_____

5. _____

_____

Use Action Words In Your Brand Promise

Your brand promise is what customers will receive when they experience or use your product or service **EVERY** time! It is what you will deliver, how you or your brand will act. Include action words in your brand promise. Here a few to consider:

Action Words:

Customizing	Removing
Growing	Distributing
Delivering	Connecting
Adding	Accommodating
Giving	Revealing
Leading	Building
Striving	Lifting
Taking	Accenting
Accessorizing	Creating
Achieving	Acknowledging
Developing	Changing
Fulfilling	Gratifying
Merchandising	Entertaining
Increasing	Appearing
Reducing	Arranging
Practicing	Operating
Improving	Exciting
Bringing	Making
Showing	Selling
Helping	Finishing
Understanding	Training

Build Your Brand Promise

Your brand promise will tell your customers what they receive as a result of using your product or service. Your brand promise should be short (5 to 10 words), simple, and easy to remember. A good brand promise can also be used as an advertising tag line.

Brand Promise Examples:

"Good to the last drop" ~ Maxwell House Coffee

"The world's most refreshing beer"~Coors Light

"Melts in your mouth, not in your hand"~M&M Candies

"The quicker picker upper"~Bounty Paper Towel

"Healthy, beautiful smiles for life"~Crest Toothpaste

"Play. Laugh. Grow"~Fisher Price Toys

"Finger-lickin' good"~Kentucky Fried Chicken

"Visine gets the red out"~Visine Eye Drops

"For the person who has everything, we have everything else"~The Sharper Image

Sample Brand Promise:

Business, product, or service: Posh SheEO.com (online business accessories store for women)

Background information and Why created? Provide functioning, fashionable and unique business accessories for women. Accessories that allow a CEO, CLO (Chief Life Officer) to show her feminine side while conducting business. Accessories such as: rhinestone writing pens and pencils, business bags reflecting the latest designer styles; colorful tablet cases with jewel embellishments, colorful planners and pad folios with jewel embellishments; rhinestone business card cases, etc. Some accessories are reflective of other cultures such as shape and materials.

Brand Promise: Accessorizing business decision making with global style and feminine flair!

Build Your Brand Promise

Start crafting your brand promise. Remember your brand promise should be short (5 to 10 words), simple, and easy to remember. Developing a brand promise statement is a process and should not be attempted in a few short hours! The best brand statements are reflected upon over several days. Create a brand promise statement and read it and allow it to "sink in." Reflect on the statement and see if it can be improved. Start with 2-3 rough drafts and substitute words and phrases during each draft. Your brand promise statement may require 5 rough drafts. Refer to the previous pages (1 through 7) to assist you.

Ready, set, go!

Brand Promise Statement Draft #1:

_____

_____

_____

Brand Promise Statement Draft #2:

_____

_____

_____

Final Brand Promise Statement:

_____

_____

_____

3. Brand Attributes

These are words—think talking points—from your brand promise that tells what you do well.

_____

_____

_____

_____

_____

_____

_____

_____

4. Brand Category

A brand category is a generic classification of products grouped by similar goods and services. Your brand category helps you focus on where you are competing for customers and where you're not. _Consult the list on pages 34 and 35 to find your business category._ Try to dominate your category.

Example:
Posh ShEO is in the category of Merchants (Retail)

_____

_____

Brand Categories

Use the list below to find your category based on your type of business.

Category	Type of Business
Automotive	Auto Accessories, Auto Dealers (New and Used), Detail and Car wash, Gas Stations, Motorcycle Sales and Repair, Rental and Leasing Service, Repair and Parts Towing
Business Support and Supplies	Consultants, Employment Agency, Marketing and Communications, Office Supplies, Printing and Publishing
Computers and Electronics	Computer Programming and Support, Consumer Electronics and Accessories
Construction and Contractors	Architects, Landscape Architects, Engineers and Surveyors, Blasting and Demolition, Building Materials and Supplies, Construction Companies, Electricians, Engineer, Survey, Environmental Assessments, Inspectors, Plaster and Concrete Plumbers, Roofers
Education	Adult and Continuing Education, Early Childhood Education, Educational Resources, Other Educational
Entertainment	Artists, Writers, Event Planners and Supplies, Golf Courses, Movies, Productions
Food and Dining	Desserts, Catering and Supplies, Fast Food and Carry Out, Grocery, Beverage and Tobacco, Restaurants
Health and Medicine	Acupuncture, Assisted Living and Home Health Care, Audiologist, Chiropractic, Clinics and Medical Centers, Dental, Diet and Nutrition, Laboratory, Imaging and Diagnostic

Brand Categories

Use the list below to find your category based on your type of business.

Category	Type of Business
	Massage Therapy, Mental Health, Nurse, Optical, Pharmacy, Drug and Vitamin Stores, Physical Therapy, Physicians and Assistants, Podiatry, Social Worker, Animal Hospital, Veterinary and Animal Surgeons
Home and Garden	Antiques and Collectibles, Cleaning, Crafts, Hobbies and Sports, Flower Shops, Home Furnishings, Home Goods, Home Improvements and Repairs, Landscape and Lawn Service, Pest Control, Pool Supplies and Service, Security System and Services
Legal and Financial	Accountants, Attorneys, Financial Institutions, Financial Services, Insurance, Other Legal
Manufacturing, Wholesale, Distribution	Distribution, Import/Export, Manufacturing, Wholesale
Merchants (Retail)	Cards and Gifts, Clothing and Accessories, Department Stores, Sporting Goods General, Jewelry, Shoes
Miscellaneous	Civic Groups, Funeral Service Providers and Cemeteries, Miscellaneous, Utility Companies
Personal Care and Services	Animal Care and Supplies, Barber and Beauty Salons, Beauty Supplies, Dry Cleaners and Laundromats, Exercise and Fitness, Massage and Body Works, Nail Salons, Shoe Repairs, Tailors

Brand Categories

Use the list below to find your category based on your type of business.

Category	Type of Business
Real Estate	Agencies and Brokerage, Agents and Brokers, Apartment and Home Rental, Mortgage Broker and Lender, Property Management, Title Company
Travel and Transportation	Hotel, Motel and Extended Stay, Moving and Storage, Packaging and Shipping, Transportation, Travel and Tourism

5. Brand Positioning

This is a one sentence statement that tells how you differ from, or are better than your competition. This is the message you plan to put into the minds of potential customers when they think about your business, product, or service.

Example:

PoshShEO has the largest selection of business accessories that represent the feminine side of business.

_____

_____

_____

_____

_____

6. Brand Anchors

This is the evidence you supply to back up your promise (testimonials from customers, clients). This information is vital to your marketing efforts.

_____

_____

_____

_____

_____

Bootstrap Branding: An Entrepreneur's Guide to Building a Brand With Limited Finances

chapter 5

Ready, Set, Brand!
(with a bootstrap budget)

Bootstrap Branding Tip #1:

Start Branding...for **FREE!** Become your own Brand Ambassador. A brand ambassador is a positive, knowledgeable spokesperson whose purpose is to increase business and promote products/services. Brand ambassadors can be consumers, friends, family, or business owners.

It is **YOUR** job as the brand ambassador for your business to make your business known! In order to increase your business and promote products/services you must **ALWAYS** be prepared and willing to tell anyone and everyone about your business. A good brand ambassador will remind (re-tell) people that you exist and what you do. Consider the act of being a brand ambassador as creating advertising buzz for your business. What does advertising do? It informs consumers that a business/product/service exists. You, as your own brand ambassador are creating advertising buzz for your business and you are advertising for **FREE!**

Being a brand ambassador can lead to collaborations and opportunities that yield an increase in business, sales, and revenue. Did you know Krispy Kreme Doughnuts was built with brand ambassadors?

Prepare to Be Your Own Brand Ambassador
Plan What to Say and Say it Consistently:
1. State the name of your business
2. State why your business/product/service is needed and the problem it solves
3. Where it can be purchased (website, store)
4. How you can be contacted (phone, email, social media)

As a Brand Ambassador, You Should:
Talk. You know your business best. You are the "go to expert" regarding your business. Tell everyone you know and meet about your business. Take advantage of social media. Create a positive, informative social media presence for your business.

Being a brand ambassador is not only "talking up" your business to everyone who will listen but representing **EVERYTHING** about your business. You are a living definition, example of your business. In other words, if you own a business, ACT like you own a business!

Educate. YOU ARE YOUR BUSINESS! You represent your business. For example, when my aunt (who has been a hair salon owner and operator for almost 50 years) gave me advice on how to find a hair stylist in my new city she said to look at the stylist's hair. The way she takes care of her hair will let me know how she will take care of my hair.

Attitude. If your business delivers "service with a smile" then you can't frown or be grumpy towards your customers, the grocery store cashier, or the person at the gas pump next to you. **EVERYONE** is a potential customer and your current customers are **ALWAYS** watching you!

Actions. So be careful and keep yourself "in check" in every situation and circumstance. When you feel the urge to "go off" on the wait staff or server that got your order wrong remember your actions are a reflection of business.

Attire. Do you realize your dress educates others on how you want to be approached? You **MUST** dress to reflect your business. What you wear will educate others about your business. Remember that **EVERY** public appearance is an interview (quick run to the store, errands, post office). Assess your dress, correct yourself before you walk out the door!

❖ As the brand ambassador your attitude, actions, and attire **MUST** reflect your brand promise, product or service constantly!

❖ As the brand ambassador you **MUST** look, act, and make decisions that represent **EVERYTHING** your business is, believes, and stands for!

Okay Brand Ambassador, your branding plan is complete now let's get to work! Here are the basic essentials you will need to start branding your business:

❖ a logo

❖ colors to represent your business

❖ business cards

❖ envelopes

❖ letterhead (for printing letters, invoices, receipts)

❖ retail items (shopping bags, gift boxes, take out containers, tissue paper, product tags)

❖ shipping items (envelopes, boxes, shipping labels, packing tape, tissue paper, shipping lists, invoices)

What is a logo? According to *businessdictionary.com* a logo is a recognizable and distinctive graphic design, stylized name, unique symbol, or other device for identifying an organization. It is affixed, included, or printed on all advertising, buildings, communications, literature, products, stationery, and vehicles. A logo is also called a brand identifier and it is the "heart and soul" of your brand that represents and defines your business.

Bootstrap Branding Tip #2:

Great logos develop over time so start simple. Your first logo can be your business name but created in a unique way. Research different logos that only use words. Find two to three that you like and use for inspiration. You may also use a combination of words and a graphic. Create your logo in black and white first! This will make sure your logo is strong without color. It will be more versatile if is strong in black and white.

Examples of word logos:

Examples of combination word and graphic logos:

Doodles page

Bootstrap Branding: An Entrepreneur's Guide to Building a Brand With Limited Finances

Doodles page

Bootstrap Branding: An Entrepreneur's Guide to Building a Brand With Limited Finances

Bootstrap Branding Tip #3:

Contact your local community college or university design class and ask them to design a logo for you. This is a great way to get a good design free. Design students are eager for the opportunity to have work created for a real client/business in their portfolio. As payment you will need to provide them with printed samples of the logo used on business cards, envelopes, etc.

Bootstrap Branding Tip #4:

Branding Colors: Select 2-3 colors, no more than 3 that will be used constantly and consistently to represent your business, product, or service. You can start with one or two of your favorite colors. You want to make sure that one of your colors is dark enough to be seen on white paper. You may find that your product or business category will dictate a color. For example a lawn cutting service may dictate the color green (grass) and brown (dirt).

Once you select your colors you want to have a representation of those colors with you at all times. You want to write down your color selections. Remember good branding is about consistency. A great way to find color swatches that represent your branding is to visit your local home improvement store. You will find great color swatches in the paint department. These swatches are durable

and can be carried easily in an envelope or small binder. I prefer the single swatch cards. This prevents me from cutting the one color I need off of the cards. You don't want to confuse your color selections. Only carry with you the two or three colors that represent your brand.

Apply Colors to Logo. Once you have decided on your brand colors make sure the colors are applied to your logo.

Notes

Bootstrap Branding Tip #5:

Make sure you place your logo and brand colors on your business cards. Here arc few other things to consider placing your logo on: envelopes, invoices, shopping bags, tissue paper, ink pens, pencils, coffee mugs, coffee sleeves, t-shirts, tote bags. If branding items other than your business cards, envelopes, and invoices are far beyond your budget then simply brand with your brand colors. For example, if red is one of your brand colors go to your favorite local dollar store and purchase red pens, pencils, and tissue paper to use instead.

Bootstrap Branding Tip #6:

Make sure you purchase a small 3-ring binder from your favorite dollar store complete with at least 1 pocket. This is a perfect size to carry with you at all times. Place your logo, color swatches, extra business cards and a list of all other BIY (Brand It Yourself) items. Make sure you list the name of the item, what you used it for, the specific location where you purchased it, the price of the item for future reference.

Bootstrap Branding Tip #7:

Everything you use for your business should always have your business name and all of your contact information. This is especially important for folders, envelopes, packaging (shopping bags, boxes). Your branding speaks on your behalf in your absence. In other words, let your branding make it easy for customers to contact you for more information, make an appointment, or make a repeat purchase.

Here are a few BIY (Brand It Yourself) Examples:

❖ Labels with the logo are applied to the product bag

❖ Labels in color are applied to scrapbooking paper found at your local craft store to create a product hang tag

❖ Red bags are used for small items. A sticker with the logo is applied to each bag

Brand it Yourself (BIY) Tips:

❖ Ask family and friends to help.

❖ Be consistent.

❖ Create an example to follow first (where the label goes)

❖ Careful attention to detail.

❖ No visible glue.

❖ Have items professionally cut at your office supply print department or purchase a personal trimmer.

❖ Take your color swatches to compare colors for accuracy. If a color is noticeably different this can cause confusion with your brand.

❖ Use printable labels. Avery© brand has created several labels specifically for the small business owner.

❖ Use pens, pencils that are your brand colors. These pens and pencils should be plain if possible.

❖ Select envelopes in one of your colors instead of white.

❖ Shop the dollar store office and gift area for paper, bags, tissue paper and boxes. Once you find your brand colors stock up!

❖ Select one office supply store print department and visit this one only. The associates will get to know you and they will operate like your "staff." They will understand your standards, likes and dislikes.

Happy Branding!
(with a bootstrap budget)

Connect with me, Dr. Vickie VanHurley, The Design Doc via the Internet and social media.

✈ thedesigndoc1@gmail.com

⏻ www.thedesigndocshop.ecwid.com

📷 thedesigndoc

🐦 TheDesignDoc

f facebook.com/vickie.vanhurley

in linkedin.com/in/drvickievanhurley

Notes

Bootstrap Branding: An Entrepreneur's Guide to Building a Brand With Limited Finances

Notes

Bootstrap Branding: An Entrepreneur's Guide to Building a Brand With Limited Finances

Doodles page

Bootstrap Branding: An Entrepreneur's Guide to Building a Brand With Limited Finances

Doodles page

Bootstrap Branding: An Entrepreneur's Guide to Building a Brand With Limited Finances

Brand It Yourself (BIY) Product Gallery and Shopping List

The quickest and easiest way to brand your product is to identify it with labels. I use and highly recommend Avery© brand labels. There are other brands but Avery© provides quality products. Avery© also offers templates online (avery.com) that makes adding your logo and information to labels easy. Consider printing on a clear label for a direct printed look.

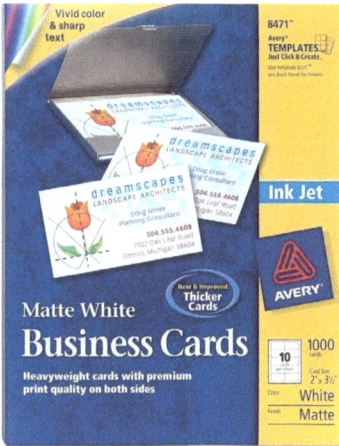
© 2016 www.avery.com

© 2016 www.avery.com

© 2016 www.avery.com

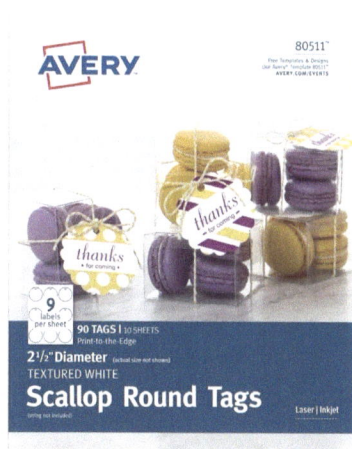
© 2016 www.avery.com

Bootstrap Branding: An Entrepreneur's Guide to Building a Brand With Limited Finances

For additional branding options consider using specialty paper or ribbon as part of your branding. Paper and ribbon can add color to your branding efforts without additional printing costs. For example, you can cut out shapes and apply the Avery© label to create a colorful product price tag or attach a ribbon to your packaging with a label. Remember to look for store sales. Sale prices always keep BIY (Brand It Yourself) items affordable!

Be sure to invest in quality adhesive for gluing paper and ribbon to your products or packaging. I use and recommend 3M Scotch© brand permanent adhesives (glue and tape). I prefer the solid stick glue over the liquid or gel to prevent wrinkling the paper or ribbon. Consider using pre-made packaging and add branding elements (labels with your logo, ribbon, etc.). Remember to visit the clearance section of your favorite arts and crafts store weekly for BIY (Brand It Yourself) items. Remember to purchase for the future especially clearance items to build up a BIY inventory. Some key items may be available at your favorite dollar store. You never want to find yourself without the necessary tools to brand your product or business.

BIY Branding Examples
(Brand It Yourself)

© 2016 www.avery.com

© 2016 www.avery.com

© 2016 www.avery.com

© 2016 www.avery.com

© 2016 www.avery.com

© 2016 Sustainable Packaging Industries
www.s-packaging.com

Bootstrap Branding: An Entrepreneur's Guide to Building a Brand With Limited Finances

www.ingramcontent.com/pod-product-compliance
Lightning Source LLC
Chambersburg PA
CBHW041711200326
41518CB00001B/156